A Time Will Come

Dennis J. Billy, C.Ss.R.

En Route Books and Media, LLC
Saint Louis, MO

Make the time

En Route Books and Media, LLC
5705 Rhodes Avenue
St. Louis, MO 63109

Cover credit: Sebastian Mahfood

Copyright © 2024 Dennis J. Billy, C.Ss.R.

ISBN-13: 979-8-88870-188-1
Library of Congress Control Number: 2024939834

No part of this book may be reproduced, stored in a retrieval system, or transmitted in any form, or by any means, electronic, mechanical, photocopying, or otherwise, without the prior written permission of the author.

For all who search.

Not all those who wander are lost.
J. R. R. Tolkien

Table of Contents

So Very Bleak	1
Why?	2
Much Depends	3
What Should Not	5
What to Say	6
Perhaps	7
My Fears	9
Alone	10
The Fear of Fear	12
The Good Lord	13
The Unraveling	14
The Unfolding	15
There Are Times	16
When?	17
Something More	18
There Are Moments	19
The Truth Is	21
Perspective	26
On Your Behalf	27
The Good News	31
The Gospel Narrative	32
Born in a Cave	33

This Christmas Night!	34
Where Are You?	36
Bartimaeus	38
Will See You Through	40
A Deeper Meaning	41
There Is a Depth	42
A Time Will Come	43
I Do Not Know	44
Suffering	45
Will Always Be	47
After That	50
All Are Welcome	51
Along the Way	53
Also Within	55
The Darkest Night	56
Take to Heart	57
Another Day	58
The Dawn	59
As a Child	61
When I Was Young	62
Summer	63
As He Sees	64
As It Unfolds	65
As the Sun	66
As Things Go	67

Become	68
Being	69
Believe	70
Blinded	71
Cancer	72
Candle	73
Come, Lord Jesus	74
COVID-19	76
Darkness	77
The Dawn	79
Twilight	80
Lazarus	81
Destiny	82
Do Not Be Afraid	84
Good Friday	85
Faith	86
Will Miss	87
Finding My Way	89
Finding Our Way	90
Follow Me	92
Forever!	94
Friends	97
From Whom It Comes	99
Easter	100
Grace	101

Grateful	102
I Believe	103
To Find My Way	104
I Long	106
I Stand in Awe	107
I Walk	109
If I Knew	110
With God's Help	111
My Wildest Dreams	112
In Hope	113
The Day Dwindles	115
In the Coming Day	116
With the Rising	118
Still to Come	120
The Day Beyond	123
The Gateway	124
In the End	125
In the Everywhere	126
In the Next	128
Insight	130
Of My Soul	131
Into the Night	132
When I Awake	134
Into the Unknown	135
Into the World Beyond	136

Is to Come 138
Life Eternal 139
Light My Journey 142
The Passing Day 143
My Friend 144
Something New 145
So Much More 146
Our Evasive God 147
The Life Beyond 148
Only You 149
Listening 150
Silence 151
Silence Yourself 152
Stillness 153
Solitude 154
What a Gift! 155
Reverence 156
Will You Join Me? 157
Still We Search 159
On the Move 161
Where Are You Going? 163
Trust 165
The Virtues 166
The Search 167
Our Journey 168

Our Journey's End 170
To Come 171
Peace of Mind 173
Memories 174
So Many Others 175
When the Light 176
Yet to Come 177
After Easter 178
Wherever the Spirit Leads 180
Of the Universe 181
Without Counting the Cost 183
When You Are 185
Your Return 186
With Gratitude 187
Mary 188

So Very Bleak

We war against each other,
From lack of trust.
The more we build trust,
The more will the ravages
Of war disappear.
Let us strive to build trust
Among ourselves,
Our communities,
Our nations,
Our world.
The alternative
Is all so very bleak.

Why?

Why do we do this!
Why do we go the war!
Why do we invade
And kill
Women and children!
Why must we
Sink,
Devolve,
Into our
Animal natures?
There are no answers,
At least in this life.
Let us hope and pray
That violence
Will one day,
Come to an end
And that
Peace may flourish.

Much Depends

Much depends
On how we look
At Life,
How we interpret,
What we see
And do not see.
Much depends
On our attitude
Toward Life,
Toward ourselves,
And toward others.
Much depends.
So much depends,
So very much depends
On you!
Yes, you!
And you alone!
Yes!
You alone!
Look inside yourself
And confront
The goodness
And, yes,
The ugliness within.
Look inside yourself.
Ponder what
You see there,
So that you
Can peer
Outside yourself
And see
With different eyes,

With eyes
That pierce
The false identifications
We make
That hinder us,
Prevent us,
Even smother us,
From reaching
And attaining
Our true goal!
Much depends,
So very much
Depends
On where
You are
Coming from
And where
You have been.
So much depends
On how you choose
To engage
The world
Around you.
So much depends,
So very much depends—
On you!

What Should Not

There are times
When one
Needs to share,
But there are
Other times
When one needs
To stay quiet
And discern
What needs
To be shared—
And what
Should not.

What to Say

Sometimes I don't know what to say.
I want to say something
But cannot find the right words.
At such times, I often feel awkward,
Small, out of touch, irrelevant.
In the midst of such feelings,
I sense a small voice rising up within me.
It is a still voice, a quiet voice,
And it tells me that sometimes
Silence is the best response
A person can make, especially
In moments of uncertainty.
Being quiet at such times
Is a gift, not a drawback.
Being silent, yet present
To another's pain may very well be
The best response one could ever give.

Perhaps

I am grateful
That I exist,
In the universe
And in all that
Surrounds me.
I am grateful
That I exist
In all things
That surround
And encompass me.
I am grateful
From where
I have come
And to where
I am going.
I am grateful
For you,
My friend,
Wherever
You come from.
I would like
To sit down
With you,
Break bread
With you,
And explore
Our differences.
Only then
Will you and I
know what
Divides us.
Only then

Will we begin
To understand
What unites us.
So, let us
sit down,
Talk
And pray,
In our own way,
Together,
In silence.
Perhaps we
Are more
Like one another
Than we
Ever knew.
Perhaps—-
Just perhaps.

My Fears

I am afraid
My fears
May take hold
And lead me
To places
I'd rather not go.
I hope
They do not
But am afraid
Nonetheless.
Such are
The difficulties
I face,
Or shall I say,
We face,
Both you and I
Day by day,
Hour by hour,
Minute by minute,
Second by second,
Until my fears,
Your fears,
Our fears,
Become themselves,
Take root in our hearts,
Wound us,
Taunt us,
Bewilder us,
And do their damage.

Alone

I freely admit
That I have
Been lonely
At times,
Many times,
Many, many times!
But I also
See
That the Lord
Works
Through those
Who seek
To be present
To those
Who have not.
I am not afraid
To be alone.
It is a gift
For you
And for me.
It is a gift
For the Church
And a gift
To me.
It is
A gift
For Christ's
Mystical Body
To which
We all
Belong.
It is

A gift
To rejoice in
And humbly
Kneel before
The Lord
In gratitude
For the gift
Of Life—-
We are never
Ever
Alone!

The Fear of Fear

Fears lurk within me in the unseen crevices of my soul,
Festering there, pushing their way into awareness,
Reeking havoc, taking their toll, clawing at my spirit,
Never letting go: unfounded fears, irrational cries from the deep,
Dwelling beneath my consciousness, overwhelming my sense of self,
Coming to mind without asking, demanding things uncalled for,
Disturbing threats, unsettling warnings, futile scenarios of doom,
Dragging me down, besieging me, defeating me, destroying me.
Lost would I be without the fear of fear to summon my courage
And help me face the shadows cast by the sun on the rising world.

The Good Lord

I am afraid
Of what
Lies before me,
But I am not
Intimidated,
Not by any means!
My safety,
My comfort,
My salvation,
Relies not on you,
Or me,
But on the
Good Lord.

The Unraveling

The world we live in
Defies our deepest values.
Beware of its influence.
It can lead you
Where you do not
Want to go.
It can sway you,
Bleed you,
Unravel you,
Blind you,
Paralyze you,
Until you
No longer
Recognize yourself
As yourself,
And have lost sight
Of your deepest
Desires,
Longings,
and aspirations.

The Unfolding

I will die,
And you will die.
Our destinies remain
Uncertain.
All we can do
Is trust
Or not trust—
This we can do,
Or not do.
The rest is out of our hands,
As our singular story unfolds.

There Are Times

There are times
When I feel
All alone.
I imagine
Everyone
Feels that way
From time to time.
Loneliness
Is a part of Life.
You and I
Will never
Be able to
Evade it,
Let alone
Overcome it.
The best
We can do
Is accept it
And see through it.
Loneliness
Is the gateway
To Solitude.
Embrace it.
Peer through it.
Allow it to tame itself
And thrive,
So that you
May grow in
The treasures
It bestows.

When?

We need
To get in touch
With our common
Humanity.
Otherwise,
We will simply
Look upon
One another
As adversaries.
Cain and Abel
All over again.
When will
We ever learn?

Something More

I yearn for something more,
And that something is more
Than what I can imagine,
Or fathom,
Or understand.
It is a something
That draws me
Beyond myself
Beyond this present life,
Beyond what I can see,
Beyond my hopes,
Beyond my dreams.
It is a something,
No, a someone,
Who calls me
To Himself,
Who calls me home
To rest in His Presence
And delight in His company.

There Are Moments

There are moments
when I experience
A downward pull
In Life,
One that drags
Me down
And leaves me
To wallow
In self-pity,
In my failures,
Sins, and human frailties.
I find myself,
At such times,
Influenced by this pull
Of becoming lesser
Rather than greater,
Of becoming
What I know
Deep down inside
I was not
Called to be,
And what
I had hoped
One day
To become.
I resist this pull
But try as I may,
I cannot overcome it.
There is only
One solution.
There is only
One answer.

There is only
One Person
Who can heal me
Of my sins!
And we know,
Even if unconsciously,
Who that is.
There is
Little difference
Between you
And me,
Between self
And other.
Let us bow down
Before the Presence
Of the Lord,
The Creator
Of the world
And all it contains!
And open
Our hearts
To Him,
The Lord
Of the Universe!

The Truth Is

(I)

No one understands what Truth is anymore!
Pilate's question, "What is Truth?"
Remains with us to this day.
SO....
What is Truth?
What do you believe it to be?
Will you live your life by it?
Will you follow its star?
Will you navigate its signs
And follow where it leads?
Or will you?
I wonder...
Don't deceive yourself.
Ponder your options.
Think it through.
Make your choice.
Decide.
Because if you don't,
You will be deceiving others
And you will also
Be deceiving yourself.

(II)

So, tell me.
Are you living by many truths
Or one truth?
Are you a divided, fragmented person
As most of us are?
I know I am

(I am ashamed to say),
And I live my life
Each day
Asking God
To help me
Bridge that gap
Between who I am
And who He envisions me to be.
But what about you?
Are you satisfied with your life?
Are you happy?
Do you find yourself
Yearning for something more?
If, so, you're in good company.
Welcome to the human race!

(III)

So let me ask you.
What is Truth?
Or what is YOUR Truth?
What is it really?
How do you live it?
Embody it?
How do you express it
By the life you live?
What really matters to you?
What are the real truths that you live by?
Can you identify them?
Delineate them?
List them?
Enunciate them?
Examine yourself.
Probe.

Delve beneath your idea of yourself.
Get in touch with you true self.
Move from you false self
To your true self,
So that you can be yourself
Before the Lord.
Go beneath.
Delve.
Take a deep breath.
Ask all the questions you wish,
But allow your spirit to breathe:
In and out.
Again,
And again...
You will certainly have questions
We all have questions.
To some, we have answers,
Others remain shrouded in mystery.

(IV)

Such questions need to be answered.
And they will be
In God's good time.
If you think you yourself
Can answer them,
You are wasting your time.
Don't kid yourself.
You cannot have it both ways.
There is a struggle in this life
Between the spirit and the flesh,
Between male and female,
Between the individual and community,
Between the one and the many.

This very struggle is going on also within your soul.
At this present moment.
Recognize it.
Admit it.
Embrace it.
Open your heart to your wounds.
Bring them to the surface.
Allow them to breathe.
Allow them to be themselves.
Bring them to your desire for Eternity.
Yet, still, recognize that that is a place
To which you cannot go,
At least by your own willing,
Because you are not worthy
And never will be.
SO!!!

(V)

Humble yourself before your very Existence,
The Source of your Being.
Talk to Him
Befriend Him,
As best you can
Don't run away.
Try!
Spend time
With yourself.
Discover your real self,
Who is rooted in
The Source of all Being!
And Who holds you,
From the moment of your conception,
From the time of your birth,

Now and always,
Close to His heart,
Forever and ever,
Amen!

Perspective

Look beyond the sky above,
Beyond the sun and moon,
Beyond the stars and planets,
Beyond the darkness and emptiness of space,
Beyond our galaxy and those beyond it,
Beyond every black hole,
Beyond life and death,
Beyond what is beyond,
Beyond even that—
Then start looking back.

On Your Behalf

I wake up.
I dawdle,
I shower.
I eat.
I face the world.
I encounter
Life
And Life
Encounters me.
I am wounded.
I am hurt.
I hurt others.
I wound,
And am wounded.
I feel lost,
And seek
My way home.
I look inside
Myself,
And ask
Myself,
Why is this
Happening!
I sit in
The Silence
Of my grief,
And hear
Deep within
My soul,
A quiet,
Whispering

Voice,
Saying,
"Do not
Be afraid.
I have
Been with you
All along.
Do not fear
The wounds
Of your Life's
Journey.
Do not fear
Your weaknesses,
Your sins,
Or your mistakes.
Do not fear
What others might say,
Or what I might say
Of you.
Do not be afraid,
Least of all,
Do not
Be afraid
Of Death!
Do not fear
Its Dark Embrace!
Do not be
Afraid
Of Him,
Or Her,
Or It,
Or whatever
It may be!
I have conquered

Death
For now
And all eternity!
In my Life,
In your Life,
In the Life
Of your loved ones,
And for so many more!
Try to look
At Life
(And Death),
As I see it,
As I have always
Seen it,
And forever will —-
I entered your
World
To become
One of you.
I have suffered
With you,
Rejoiced with you,
And cried with you.
I have lived
Your deepest fears.
I have been through
Whatever you may
Be asked
To go through.
Even Death!
So, do not afraid!
I have conquered
Death.
By confronting It,

Embracing It,
And defeating It!
And It,
So very
Long ago,
Because
Of Its encounter
With me
Has relinquished
Control
Over you,
And has let
You go—-
All because of me!
So do not
Fear.
Perfect Love
Drives out
All Fear.
Be consoled—-
I am with you
Until the end of Time!"

The Good News

Such is humanity's plight:
Our minds are darkened,
Our wills weakened,
Our emotions out of sync,
Our bodies destined for the grave.
The Good News is that
God entered our world
To reverse this trend.
Because of Him,
Our graves will open,
Our bodies rise,
Our emotions will be ordered,
Our wills strengthened,
Our minds enlightened,
And we shall enter
Into the presence of God
As His precious sons and daughters.

The Gospel Narrative

The Gospel narrative
Must be spoken,
Written,
Interpreted,
Believed,
Embraced,
Lived,
Prayed,
Enjoyed,
And shared.

Born in a Cave

Born in a cave,
An infant, wrapped
And swaddled,
Sleeps in a manger,
As night descends,
And the cold air chills,
As the angels sing,
And the shepherds hasten,
As a distant star leads,
And the wise men follow,
As Joseph dreams,
And Mary ponders,
As the Word becomes flesh,
And a wounded world hopes,
As Love shines forth,
And Darkness dwindles,
Then vanishes,
Both now and forever,
From every lonely
And forsaken place
In the hidden caves
And secret crevices
Of my hungry, yearning heart.

This Christmas Night!

This Christmas night!
This glorious night!
The night when history
Comes to its head
And the turning point
Of all existence
Humbly sets
The course of Life
Upon God's chosen path.
This Christmas night!
This holy night!
This glorious night!
When divinity and humanity
Meet in the fragility
Of a newborn child
Born in a manger,
Fresh from his mother's womb,
Away from home,
Crying,
Longing to be held,
Comforted,
And fed,
Resting in a trough
In swaddling clothes,
Kept warm by the breath
Of animals,
Helpless and in need,
Who comes to us,
By His simple presence,
Proclaiming a Kingdom
Yet to come,
But already in our midst!

This night!
This holy night!
This silent night!
This night of nights!
Proclaims
That we are not
Unwanted, abandoned orphans
Set adrift
In a sea of mindless atoms,
But that God,
Himself,
His Father,
Our Father,
Has given us
His Word
And sent
His Son
To dwell among us,
Redeem us
In the flesh,
And help us find
Peace of mind,
Stillness of spirit,
Tranquility of heart,
And the freedom
To accept His call
To be His sons
And daughters—-
And live life accordingly.

Where Are You?

I
Where are you?
I mean,
Where are you really?
Where are you
In your relationship
To your final end?
In your relationship with
Your deepest dreams,
In your relationship
With your God,
In relationship with your neighbors,
In your relationship with those around you,
In your relationship with yourself,
Your deepest self,
Your one, true self?
Where are you?

II
Ponder your life
Ponder your afterlife.
Ponder the path
Before you.
After all,
In the end,
God is the one thing,
The one Person,
The only Person
Who matters.

III

So reflect on
Your past.
Embrace your present,
Ponder your future.
Let go of your life.
Let Him take control,
And see the miracles
That are sure to happen.

Bartimaeus

What can a blind man do
But sit and beg?
I could not see
What others saw,
But I could hear,
And I could speak!

So there I was
On the roadside
At the Jericho gate
With a bowl at me feet,
Asking for whatever
Anyone would give me.

I then heard a roar of voices,
And I knew a crowd was passing.
I asked what it was all about,
And someone said that
Jesus of Nazareth
Was coming.

I could hear,
And I could speak,
So I raised my voice
And shouted out,
"Jesus, Son of David,
Have pity on me!

They tried to quiet me,
But I would not be silenced.
"Jesus, Son of David!
Have pity on me!"

Jesus stopped
And called me over.

I threw aside my cloak
And went up to him.
He asked me what I wanted,
And I told him
Without any hesitation,
"Rabboni, I want to see."

He looked into my eyes
And said, "Your faith has healed you."
And from that moment on,
I was able not only
To hear and speak,
But also see.

Will See You Through

There are times
When things go well,
And there are times
When things do not.
Rather than rejoicing
In the good times
And lamenting the bad,
Try to sense the Lord's
Quiet presence
In your life,
For He is someone
Who tests
And disciplines us,
As a father does
To his son
Or daughter.
Do not be afraid
To face
Whatever Life
Throws at you.
Rely on the Lord
At all times.
He will see
You through.

A Deeper Meaning

Night falls.
The moon rises.
Darkness descends.
I close my eyes
And fall asleep.
I dream dreams
That take me
To another world,
A hidden world,
One beneath
My consciousness,
That reveals to me
The deeper meaning
Of my conscious life,
My hidden life,
And unfolding future.

There Is a Depth

There is a depth
In the human spirit
That we have only,
Just yet, begun to mine.
To do so, we must
Be quiet and listen
To what is being spoken
Deep down within!
Listen to your dreams!
Follow them!
Do not look back.
You were tasked
And created for them!

A Time Will Come

A Time will come
When Time itself
Will change
And be transformed.
Where will you
Be at that moment?
Will you have tried
To transform Time
Or will Time
have transformed
You?

I Do Not Know

I do not know
The day or hour
When I will close my eyes
And open them no more.
I do not know
Where I will be
Or with whom,
If I will be alone
Or with others,
At home,
Or elsewhere.

I do not know
What the cause will be.
Be it an accident,
Or a disease,
Or old age.
I do not know.
I do not want to know.
Knowing would make
Living more difficult,
And dying—
No longer a great unknown.

Suffering

Why do I suffer?
Why am I going through
What my body tells me
Is happening,
But my spirit
Mind and heart
Refuse to accept
And otherwise doubt?
Why do I suffer?
Why?
There are no easy answers.
We may look
To what the experts say.
We may look
To what others tell us.
We may look
To our own experience,
And we may even look
To what Life itself
Tells us about ourselves
And the meaning
Of our lives.
Where are we to go?
With faith?
Or without it
With our loved ones?
Or without them?
With God?
Or without Him?
Such are the choices
Before us.
Let us choose wisely,

Second by second,
Minute by minute,
Hour by hour,
Day by day,
Year by year,
From dawn to dusk,
From evening to morning,
From morning till night,
From dream to dream,
From hope to hope,
Until our journey's end.

Will Always Be

I look inside
Myself
And see you,
In me,
A reflection
Of myself
(And I
In you).
I blink my eyes
And see humanity,
All of us,
Times present
And past.
I see us
Everywhere,
In all
Our wounds,
In all our
Weaknesses
And frailties,
In all our
Broken dreams
And promises,
In all
Our lost hopes
And aspirations.
I see all this!
And am tempted,
At times,
To lose heart,
And perhaps

Even despair.
Why continue?
Why go on?
Why not give in?
I listen to
These voices,
These chilling
Negative voices,
And something
Deep inside me
Says
"No!"
I will not relent!
I will fight
To the end!
I will not
Be defined
By those voices
That seek
To undercut
All that
I have lived for
And am willing
To die for!
I will not!
I believe
The day will come
When you and I
Will confront,
Struggle with,
And defeat
The demons
Within us,
And do so

Concretely,
Definitively!
Once and for all!
But I know
I can do this
Only with the help
Of Someone—-
That wounded,
Broken,
Defeated,
Dying,
Lamb,
Who has looked
Upon us,
So long ago,
Has entered
Our world
And deemed
Us worthy
To suffer
And die for us,
To lead us,
Deliver us,
And sanctify us!
Now and forever.

After That

A stranger walked by me
The other day.
And the day after that,
And the day after that,
And the day after that.

I nodded to him one day,
And he nodded back,
The day after that,
And the day after that,
And the day after that.

Then one day
We smiled at each other,
The day after that,
And the day after that,
And the day after that.

And then we became friends—
Good friends, bosom buddies—
And the day after that
Became just that:
The day after that!

All Are Welcome

We all suffer.
We all succumb
To our suffering,
We all die.
We all face
The prospect
Of Non-Being,
Of Non-Existence,
Of Nothingness,
Of Death
In all its fullness!
Yes, such is
Our Fate,
Unless we look
To Our Lord,
Our Good Lord,
Our Humble,
Yet Edifying Lord,
As He succumbs
To our suffering
For us!
For you
And for me!
This is
The Gospel message'
For Jews
And Gentiles alike:
"Come, Lord Jesus!"
Accept Him
Or reject Him;
Receive Him
Or deny Him.

There is
No compromise!
And yet,
There is openness.
As we listen—-
And there is dialogue
With one another.
What that means
For you
And for me
Remains to be seen.
Still, this is my hope—-
All are welcome!

Along the Way

I believe
This truth
Is deeply rooted
In the human psyche:
The Earthquakes,
Hurricanes
Tornadoes,
Of the outer world,
Reverberate within
And often
Wreak havoc
On the inner landscape
Of our souls.
They can cause
Deep Physical,
Psychological,
Spiritual,
And Social wounds
That enter
Our living memory
And hardly ever
Go away.
Tragedies
Are a part
Of Life
And are sure
To accompany us
Along the way.
How we respond
To them,
What we learn
From them,

And how we grow
In spite of them
Are concerns
That should concern
Each of us,
Each and every day!

Also Within

I do not wish
To live in a world
That has lost it sense
Of the sacred.
That is why
I yearn
For the Kingdom
That is to come.
Still,
In the quiet moments
Of the night,
When I listen
To the silence
And try to hear
What God
Is telling me,
I wish
To rediscover
The sacred,
Not just
Without,
But also
Within.

The Darkest Night

I look up at the night sky
And see the stars
Shining down on us
In myriad points of light.
If they could speak,
I wonder what
They would say?
I stand in awe,
And silent reverence,
Before these bright,
Burning flames
That envelop
The darkness of night.
Their untold beauty
Touches my heart
And fills it with hope
That the world will
Never, ever be
Deprived of Light—
Even in the darkest night.

Take to Heart

Take to heart the words I say.
Do not be alarmed.
There is no need to fear.
This day shall pass.
Tomorrow, the sun shall rise,
And you and I will find ourselves
In a better place.

Another Day

The sun rises.
The day begins.
I open my eyes,
And greet the dawn.
I get out of bed
And fall on my knees
To thank the Lord
For another day.

The Dawn

The Sun dips
Below the Horizon,
For the time of Dusk
Is at hand,
The movement
Of Light
Into Shadow,
That slowly dims
Into the Darkness
Of the Unknown
Has come.
As I close
My eyes
And enter into
The Myriad Mysteries
Of Sleep,
I wonder
Who knows
What the Night
Will hold?
Who knows
What the Dawn
Will bring?
Who knows
What will happen
When I open
My eyes?
Each Day
I experience
The rising and
The setting
Of the Sun,

And enter
The Land
Of my Dreams,
Where I
Am reminded
Of the Dusk
That is
To come
In my own Life,
That I myself
Must one day
Experience,
Face,
And Undergo.
I do not
Look forward
To that Dusk.
I avoid it.
Evade it.
Run from it,
As much
As possible,
But at the
Same time
Still,
There is
Something
Within me
That eagerly
Awaits
It's coming—
As I await
The Dawn.

As a Child

As a child
I couldn't wait
To grow up.
Now that I am old,
I yearn for
My younger days:
The ways of my youth
And the promise
Of a better life.

When I Was Young

When I was young
I wondered what
Old age would bring.
Now that I am old,
I look back on my past
And experience it anew.

Summer

I remember when summer
Seemed like an eternity,
And we would play outdoors
All day long.
Now summer passes
In the blink of an eye,
And what we call play
Pales in comparison.

As He Sees

I look out upon my past
And see all the people
I have encountered,
Talked with, and met,
And wonder if my
Meeting them
Made any difference
In their lives
Or in my own.
It just goes
To show that
Each human encounter,
With a mother or a father,
A brother or a sister,
A close relative,
A friend or neighbor,
Or even a complete stranger,
Is precious in the eyes
Of the Lord!
Let us open our eyes
And see
Those around us
As the Lord Himself
Sees them.

As It Unfolds

I celebrate Life!
I live it as I see fit.
I follow my conscience,
Or at least I try.
I savor each moment
And seek to live
In the present.
I have no idea
What the future holds.
To be honest,
I really don't wish
To know.
Why should I?
What good
Would that do?
Life is an adventure.
I wish to experience it
As it unfolds.

As the Sun

As the sun dips
Below the horizon,
I ponder the coming night
And peer into the darkness
That awaits me.
I close my eyes
And pray for sleep
To take me to
The land of dreams,
Where darkness
And light mingle
In the shadow
Of their opposites
And rise together
To greet the dawn
Of another world,
A better world,
The one that is
To come.

As Things Go

Things go wrong,
For sure,
And who do
We blame?
Anyone
But ourselves.
Blaming,
However,
Has its way
Of turning
Things around,
And around they
Will turn,
Until the Truth
Is uncovered
And comes to light,
And we shall be
Either mortified
Or justified!

Become

Empty yourself
Of self.
Be present
To the person
Before you.
Take off
The false self.
Listen.
Receive.
Be.
Become
Your true self
In the person
Of the other.

Being

Where do you come from?
Out of nothing?
Out of the world?
Out of your father's sperm?
Out of your mother's womb?
Where do you come from?
This is the question
We all must answer.
Where do we come from?

I believe I come from Being.
I believe I come from God.
I believe I have been created.
This is my faith.
This is the way
I live my life.
Don't challenge me
On this.
I will never relent!

Believe

To change the world
We need to change
Our hearts.
This is accomplished
One heart at a time,
Person to person,
Friend to friend,
Heart to heart.

Live the Gospel!
Follow Our Lord!
Our inner world affects
Our outer world.
Follow Him!
Leave all behind!
Don't count the cost!
Believe!

Blinded

I look at the Sun
And am blinded
By its radiance!
I look at you
And am blinded
By the radiance
Of the Divine
Shining through
You!

Cancer

I have had cancer,
That dreadful disease.
I've spent months in the hospital,
Received tons of chemo,
Relapsed twice,
Was given the talk,
Told there was nothing more
The doctors could do for me,
And by sheer circumstance
(Or Providence, as I prefer to believe),
Am alive today because of the power of prayer
And the miracle of modern medicine.
All this happened a long time ago,
And the doctors have told me I am cured.
Still, I have a sense that my cancer
Is lurking somewhere deep inside of me,
Ready to ravage me again,
As it once did so many years ago.
I live with this fear every day.
It is the new normal of my life.
I have learned to accept it,
Live with it, and even befriend it.
I have also learned that Life is precious
And should not be taken for granted.
I try to live in the present moment
With gratitude in my heart
For the gift of Life,
The love of family and friends,
And the quiet voice I hear
Deep within my heart
That all shall be well.

Candle

A candle burns.
Its light shines.
Its wax melts.
Its wick snuffs.
Its death beckons.
Its darkness looms.
Our sight blurs.
Confusion rages—
Another candle is lit.

Come, Lord Jesus

Life is hard.
It grills us
And presses
Us down
To a point
That we
Can hardly
Bear.
Such is Life.
There is
No alternative,
Except for
Our hope
In Christ,
Whose Holy Spirit
Still rules,
Albeit in
Mysterious ways,
In the midst
Of darkness
And despair,
In the midst
Of uncertainty
And unbridled
Longing!
Let us proclaim
Together
And with full voices,
The origin of our Lord,
The righteousness
And fullness
Of Jesus who is Lord

And as we await his coming,
Proclaim:
"Jesus Christ is Lord!
"Come, Lord Jesus!
Come!

COVID-19

Your ghastly figure daunt and grim we see,
Amid these corpses, still too young, once free,
Are pleading for some mercy far or near,
But you have neither mind nor heart to hear.

To science, then, we turn to here-and-now,
To seek a cure, and find for us somehow,
A way to conquer what we once denied,
A way to salvage lives and human cries.

O Leveler of Life, we know amid
The tragedy of lives and deaths, once lived,
That Christ, Our Lord, your greatest foe of all
Has conquered Death itself— and you shall fall!

Darkness

There is Darkness
In all our lives.
It envelops us,
Sickens us,
And disfigures us.
We must recognize
It's existence,
Name it,
Confront it,
Wrestle with it,
And turn it over
To God.
We cannot
Defeat this Darkness
On our own.
Only God can defeat
What we ourselves
Cannot.
Only He can do
The impossible,
Only He can
Do what we cannot.
So, get down on
Your knees and pray.
Humbly ask
The Lord
To forgive you,
To help you,
To strengthen you,
To watch over you,
And guide you,
As you struggle

To free yourself,
With God's help,
From the many ghosts
Who to this very day
Haunt you
And hound you.

The Dawn

The Sun sinks
Below the horizon,
And endures
The Night.
After a time,
It gently rises
To another Day.
As it lingers,
It mixes
With the atmosphere
Above us
And the clouds
Within our sight,
To send forth
A beautiful array
Of colorful blends
To herald in
The Dawn.

Twilight

As I enter into the twilight,
And as the twilight
Enters into me,
I wonder if what
I have seen
In this Life
Has been nothing
But total Darkness.
I wonder,
When I close my eyes,
If I will see
Or at least hope
To see,
What I had hoped
I would see
Beyond my deepest
Dreams—-
Beyond
My wildest
Imaginings,
Beyond all hope,
Beyond all sight,
Beyond all means.
I wonder?

Lazarus

After four days of decay,
They braced themselves for the stench.
Touched by the women's tears,
Moved by his love for his friend,
Jesus peered into the darkness of the cave,
And cried out, "Lazarus, come forth!"
A ghostly figured emerged,
Hands and feet bound,
Face wrapped in linen.
"Untie him and set him free!"
Death has no power
Where Love reigns supreme.

Destiny

There is Darkness
In Life,
A Darkness
So deep
It cannot
Be seen.
It lurks
Outside of us,
But also within us.
It wants
To swallow us
And lead us
Into oblivion.
The Light
On the other hand
Wishes to penetrate us
And enable us
To see what
Now
We can only see
Dimly,
As in
A mirror.
In the Life
We live,
There is Darkness
And Light.
We are left
To choose
A path
Of our own making.
Whatever path we choose,

There is no return.
Darkness or Light.
Choose wisely.
Your eternal destiny
Is at stake.

Do Not Be Afraid

Do not be afraid
About what is about
To happen.
It may be
Something
You have long
Expected,
Or not.
Do not be afraid
Of what
May come to pass,
Or what has
Already happened.
The Lord is with you.
No matter what happens.
All you need to do
Is to trust,
And ask the Lord
For the help to do so.

Good Friday

The sun stood still
As the sky grew dark,
And clouds thickened
On the horizon.
The ground shook
And the earth quaked,
As gloom covered the land
And penetrated the world's inner landscape.
Hearts trembled.
Women and children wept.
Young men and old fled in fear,
And recoiled in shame.
A solitary cross,
Flanked by two others,
The good thief and the bad,
Held a bloodied, lifeless corpus in its arms.
Suspended between night and day,
Between ground and sky,
Between heaven and earth,
Between sin and grace.
A union of God and man,
Of man and God,
Of the heart of God
And the heart of man.
This pierced and broken heart
Rent the Temple curtain in two,
And the Holy of Holies
Poured itself upon the world
To cleanse and renew it,
To heal and transform it,
To bring it back to itself,
And make it whole.

Faith

Faith leads me into darkness,
And darkness into light.
I walk with hesitation,
Searching for
The light of light,
And wondering
If I will ever find it.

Will Miss

I stand in awe
Of the world
I live in.
Despite
Its many,
(Quite obvious)
Flaws,
It is still
A place
Of searching,
Of insight,
Of discovery.
I am so
Grateful
To be a part
Of this world!
I am so
Grateful
To be alive!
To breathe!
To befriend!
To behold!
I will miss
The day
When I can
No longer
Share my
Thoughts
With you.
I will miss
The day
When you

And I
Can connect
Only through prayer.
I will miss
That day,
When I imagine,
I will be
Sorely missed,
At least for
A time,
As time passes
Into eternity—
As do we.

Finding My Way

I look into the Darkness
And see the Unknown.
I look into my Heart
And sense Another Self.
I look into my Self
And sense Someone
Drawing me,
Calling me,
Encountering me,
Challenging me,
Loving me,
And Offering me
Help,
Always Help,
Whether asked for
Or Not
Always Help—
To find my way Home.

Finding Our Way

We were made
To share
A deep
Collective
Consciousness,
An awareness
That would put
Us in touch
With one another,
Similar to what
We find
In a colony
Of ants,
Or a hive
Of bees,
Or a herd
Of buffalo.
But this
We lost
Long,
Long ago,
Due to
The sin
Of our
Forbearers,
The sin
Of human origins.

The ants
And bees,
And buffalo
Are remnants

Of our past,
Relics of
A time gone by,
Vestiges,
Traces that
God has
Left behind
To point
The way
For us to explore
And travel—
And we must
Until we find
Our journey's end
And rest in the shadow
Of our origins
And the embrace
Of the One
Who made us
Out of the nothingness
From which we came
And Who keeps us
In being.

Follow Me

There is something
We all wish to avoid,
Our mortality—-
The fact that
One day,
You and I
Will die.
You and I
Will wither
And fade,
Becoming
The dust from
Which we came
And shall return.
You and I
Will sense Death,
Avoid it,
Run from it,
Flee from it,
Deny it,
And ultimately
Face it.
But in the end,
It will embrace us!
Overwhelm us!
Consume us!
Devour us!
Destroy us!
And,
As Time goes on,
In the infinity of Space
And its limitations,

Lost in that
Dismal embrace,
There will,
In Time,
Arise
A still small voice
Crying out,
To one and all,
In the wilderness
Of our hearts—-
Your heart,
My heart,
Everyone's heart—-
"Rise up!
Listen to Me!
Look to Me!
Come to Me!
Follow Me!"

Forever!

Life passes
But to where?
As you and I
Grow old,
This question
Looms large.
The response
You and I
Can make,
Is to say
That God
Does not
Exist
And there
Is no Afterlife.
Another response,
One of many
(All of the
Others of which
Falter,
At least by
My simple reckoning!)
Is that He
Does exist
And has
Suffered for us
So that
We might
Be freed
Our sins
And liberated
From Death.

Of the two possibilities
(And the first
Fails by comparison),
I'll go with
The latter…
Why?
Because
There surely is
Something
Planted deep
Inside our hearts
That whispers,
And speaks,
And even
Shouts out—-
I am alive
And will live
Forever!
I am
A son
Or a daughter
Of God!
I believe!!!
My dear Lord.
Help my unbelief…
And to you
I say,
Encounter
Your uncertainties,
Face your doubts.
Name them.
Wrestle with them.
Look into your
Shadow side,

Lose yourself
There
And pray to God—-
For help.
Choose your destiny.
God is forever
Listening…
He is there
For you
And will
Never abandon
You,
Not ever,
Not ever,
Not ever.

Friends

I am grateful
For all of you,
Each
And
Every
One
Of you!
I am closer
To some
More
Than others,
As you are
To me
And I am
To you.
But still,
I call
Each
Of you
My friend.
Let us
Continue to
Go through
Life
Making
Friends,
Both large
And small!
And let us
Do so
In the Spirit
Of Our Lord,

Jesus Christ
Himself,
Who said,
"I no longer
Call you servants,
But friends!"
Let us
Do so
In Him,
And for Him!
For doing so
Makes His memory,
Deeply present,
To me
And to you—-
Ever willing
To share,
Ever ready
To walk
In His footsteps.

From Whom It Comes

Life does not always
Smile upon me.
There have been
Good times
And bad,
Times of joy
And others
Of great sadness.
Still, whatever
Life throws at me,
I smile
And even cry
Over the Life
I have been dealt.
Still, I do not
And will not
Ever complain.
It is a wonder
That I exist
At all.
I savor the moments
Of my Life,
The good
And the bad,
The joyful
And the sad.
I smile upon Life
And give homage
From the depths
Of my heart
To the Source
From Whom it comes.

Easter

He is Risen!
This is the crux,
The turning point
In our lives.
If you believe,
Life takes
On a whole
Different meaning.
If you do not,
Then the meaning
You find in Life
Will be very
Much diminished.

Ponder this Truth,
The Truth of Easter!
Reflect on it
And pray,
Even if you
Have doubts!
Open your heart
And ask the Lord
To open your eyes,
So that you might see
And your heart
Might feel.
Come to the Lord Jesus,
Come!
Hear Him
As He calls
Each of you
By name!

Grace

I look into my Past
And see my Future.
What I have done
Has shaped my Life
And has sent me
Into a Downward
Spiral,
Into Death,
My only Hope
My only, only Hope
Is the Grace of God!

Grateful

I sense your Presence
From one moment
To the next.
I try to stay
In the moment
But find it
So difficult
To do so.
Yet, still,
I believe,
And I sense,
You believe,
That my
Very trying
Brings joy
To your eyes.
And for this
I am grateful,
So very, very
Grateful.

I Believe

I believe in God.
I believe in Life after Death.
I believe that we are created
In God's image
And called to love one another
As God loves us.
I believe that God
Looks and smiles upon us,
As a Father looks upon His Son,
And as the Son looks toward His Father.
I believe that God believes in me,
That He loves me so much
That I am able,
With His help,
Despite my many faults,
Failings, and sins,
To find my way homeward
To Him—-
However long it takes.

To Find My Way

When night falls
My imagination quickens,
And I see things
I had never
Seen before.
I look outside
Myself
And see the troubles
That surround me,
Day by day,
Second by second,
Moment by moment,
But I also
Come
Face-to Face
With the Inward
Struggles that
No one else
Can see.
This is who
I am!
I confront myself
And I see God,
Confronting my
Inner awareness
Of what is True.
I see Him
Needling me,
Pressing me,
Confronting me!
Encountering me!
One to one,

Each to each,
Day and night,
Friend to friend,
Mourning His passing,
Encompassing
The Night,
And seeking
Daybreak!
I come before Him,
The Lord, my God,
In need
And in humility,
Asking Him
For forgiveness,
And a way forward.
Only this I ask.
Only this I seek.
Help me, Lord.
Help me
To find my way.

I Long

I long for
The long ago,
When moments passed
Without measure,
When space
Illuminated the sky,
When the sun set,
When night fell,
And the stars radiated
The Lord Most High.

I Stand in Awe

I stand in awe
Of the world
I live in.
Despite
Its many,
(Quite obvious)
Flaws,
It is still
A place
Of searching,
Of insight,
And of discovery.
I am so
Grateful
To be a part
Of this world!
I am so
Grateful
To be alive!
To breathe!
To befriend!
To behold!
I will miss
The day
When I can
No longer
Share my
Thoughts
With you
And can connect
Only through prayer.
I will miss

That day,
When I suppose
And imagine,
I will be
Sorely missed,
By family
And friends,
At least for
A time,
Or for all time.
As time passes,
As time itself passes—
And so do we.

I Walk

I walk the morning.
I walk in the afternoon.
I walk in the evening.
I walk because I need to walk.
I walk because it helps me think.
I walk because it helps me pray.
I walk because it helps me be still.
I walk because I feel I am going somewhere.
I walk because I can walk, listen,
And know that the day will come
When I will no longer be able to walk.
I do not look forward to that day,
But anticipate its coming
And hope that when it comes—
I will learn to fly.

If I Knew

If I knew
The day
I would die,
I wonder
If my life
Would be
Any different.

Not knowing
Makes me
Wonder,
If I should
Be doing
Anything
Differently.

With God's Help

The sun rises
To the break of day.
Its rays touch the earth
In rainbow colors.
And leave me speechless.
Nowhere have I ever
Encountered
Such beauty!
Nowhere have I
Ever felt this close
To God!
It makes me ponder
And reflect on
My difficult life,
My broken life,
My wandering life…
If such beauty
Was ever made
For me to behold,
How could I not
Bow my head
In thankfulness
And gratitude
To the source
From which it came,
As I hope that
Somehow,
One day,
I will find it in me,
With God's help,
To find my way home.

My Wildest Dreams

As I enter into the twilight,
And as the twilight
Enters into me,
I wonder if what
I have seen
In this Life
Has been nothing
But total Darkness.
I wonder
When I close my eyes
If I will see
Or at least hope
To see,
What I had hoped
I would see—-
Or something else,
Far beyond
My wildest dreams.

In Hope

I ponder
The root questions
Of why
I exist?
Why others exist?
Why the world exists?
Why there is existence
At all?
I ponder
All these questions,
And wonder,
As I always do,
Why I am here?
As I do so,
The only credible
Explanation
I can find
Is that,
I am not
A random
Collection of atoms,
But that
There is
Some purpose
Behind
My ordering.

That belief
Keeps me sane
And enables me
To go on
With my life,
And live
In hope.

The Day Dwindles

The day dwindles into night,
As we journey towards death
And find ourselves bathing in darkness,
Something no one wishes
To go through, let alone suffer
And embrace as one's destiny.
But we must go through it.
Go through it, we must!
For only by doing so can we
Ever hope to find ourselves
In the shadow of the One
Who suffered, bled
And died for us
Of his own accord,
So we might follow him
Accompany him,
In our lives,
In our suffering,
In our deaths—
Until our journey's end.

In the Coming Day

With the rising
Of the sun,
I open my eyes
And am grateful
For the beginning
Of yet another day.
At this moment,
I look around,
And reflect on
What I have seen
And heard,
For good
Or bad.
I open and shut
My eyes many times
Throughout the day
And try to keep
Them focused
On what is
Before me,
Beneath me,
Above me,
Beside me,
And Beyond me.
Such is Life.
Something given.
Something lost.
Something hoped for.
Something so very elusive.
At the end of each day
I close my eyes
Once more,

And ponder if,
During that time,
I understood
What I have learned
To help me
Make my way,
With you, my friends,
In the coming day.

With the Rising

With the rising
Of the sun,
I open my eyes
And am grateful
For the beginning
Of yet another day.
At this moment,
I look around,
And reflect on
What I have seen
And heard,
For good
Or bad.
I open and shut
My eyes many times
Throughout the day
And try to keep
Them focused
On what is
Before me,
Beneath me,
Above me,
Beside me,
And Beyond me.
Such is Life.
Something given.
Something lost.
Something hoped for.
Something so very elusive.
At the end of each day
I close my eyes
Once more,

And ponder if,
During that time,
I have understood
What I have learned
To help me
Make my way,
With you, my friends,
To the coming day.

Still to Come

Deep down within,
My voice is calling you.
It always has
And always will.
Come to me, I say.
Journey with me.
Not reluctantly,
Or haphazardly,
Or warmly,
Or coldly,
Or even
Against me,
Against your
Own deepest desires
And unsung hopes.
Listen to me,
Deep within
Your heart!
Follow me,
However you can.
However you will.
However you
Wish not to will,
Or not wish to will!
Whatever you will,
Whatever you say,
Whatever you believe,
However you act,
There is time,
Much time,
An Eternity
Of Time

For you
And I
To come
To know each other.
An Eternity
Of Time,
For you
And I
To seek
Each other out
And befriend
One another.
If only you
Would look to me
And follow me
To where
I am guiding you.
Because where
You are
Deep down inside
And where you
Wish and dream
Of going
Is where
I am leading you.
Yes,
To something
Far beyond
Your wildest dreams—-
To a place
I have prepared
For you
Beyond the Life
You presently know

To the One
I have prepared
For you,
To the One
That is
Still to come.

The Day Beyond

As night falls,
Sleep soothes
Our tired bodies,
Weary souls,
Restless spirits,
And broken relationships,
Bestowing momentary rest
Upon our tired,
Wounded world.
These dreams
Inhabit our unconscious minds
Bringing to the surface
Forbidden thoughts,
Forsaken hopes,
And secret lies,
Revealing to us
What was hidden,
Unmasking our unspoken fears.
They linger
At the sun's rising
And point out the way
For us to walk
Into the day,
Into the night,
Into the night
Beyond the night,
And into the day beyond.

The Gateway

Time passes.
It comes
And goes—
As do we.
Let us not
Live our lives
As slaves
To Time.
Let us
Befriend it,
Beseech it,
Deliver it,
Transform it,
By turning Chronos
Into Kairos
And Living
In the Present
Moment—
The Gateway
To Eternity.

In the End

In the end,
"All shall be well."
So said the mystic
So many centuries ago.
And her words
Reverberate
Through the soul
And down the corridors
Of time.
Do you believe them?
Do you believe
That when all is said
And done,
"All shall be well"?
If not,
Why not?
Ponder these words,
Breathe them in and out,
Reflect upon them
Make them your own,
And then wait,
Simply wait.

In the Everywhere

I am where I am,
And you are
Where you are.
God is
Where He is—-
Everywhere!
So, let us
Each seek
To encounter
One another
In the Everywhere.
Please,
Let us try!
If only you
And I
Would try
To encounter
One another
In the Everywhere—
It is a Place,
That is No-Place,
Or any Place,
A Place that
Can only be found,
If we discover ourselves
In the Everywhere
And if we try
In the present moment,
Deep within our hearts,
Deep within
Our deepest selves,
Deep within

The Anywhere
The Nowhere,
And the Everywhere
That resounds
Outward
From within,
From deep
Within the
The Place
That no one
Wants to go!
Let us go There.
Let us live There,
You and I,
For now
And forever—-
Let us live
In the Everywhere,
And let the Everywhere
Live in us!

In the Next

There is something that looms
In the back of our minds.
We don't notice it at first,
But as we grow older,
It moves more and more
To the forefront and,
As we begin to notice it,
It starts to haunt us,
And dominate our thinking.
This is something
We all must face.
If we are not careful,
It will take control of us
And force us to think
In ways we ought not.
You and I will one day die.
This is a fact.
Each of us must face
Our final moment!
When it comes,
May there be people
Around us,
Who will mourn for us,
Eulogize us,
Remember us,
And continue to love us—-
Or maybe not.
There may be no one
At all to comfort us,
Or bid us "Farewell!"
As we end our journey.
All we can do is trust,

Trust in the One
Who came to us
So that we might
Build our trust in him,
And allow him to do the same,
In this Life—
And in the next.

Insight

There is
A deeper wisdom
For those who search
And yearn
For it.
It will come
To those
Who see
That it lies
So very much
Deep within
In the fabric
Of their hearts.

Of My Soul

Night has fallen,
A full moon shines.
Stars speckle the heavens.
The planets run their course.
Wonder stirs my heart.
Awe quiets my mind.
I contemplate the evening sky
And see in it—
A reflection of my soul.

Into the Night

Come, Darkness,
Into the Gentle
Yet Silent Night,
Into the Vast
Unknown.
Come with the Certainty
Of what is Uncertain,
That what is Known
Will be Unknown.
Come, Lord,
Come.
Speak to me
Of the Loss
Of Sight,
And all my senses,
Of an ever
Deepening
Sense of
Abandonment
To the Night
Of Divine Light.
Come, Lord,
Come.
Open my eyes.
Help me to see.
Cover me with
Your Silent,
Ever Present,
And Listening
Heart.

Do not delay.
Come, Lord.
Come!

When I Awake

When I awake,
I open my eyes
To the world.
I shower,
Dress,
Eat,
And make
Myself ready
For the day
Ahead.
I do this
Because
I believe
There is
A purpose
In Life
And that I
Must willingly
And intentionally
Be a part
Of it.

Into the Unknown

Life is beautiful,
And so is Death,
At least for those
Who believe
In the Afterdeath.
I do.
That is not
To say
That I am not
Fearful
Of what
Lies beyond.
I certainly am.
Still, I embrace
That fear
And am ready
To travel
Into the Unknown,
Into the Darkness,
Into the Deep
Cloud of Unknowing,
Into the Abyss,
The Mystery
From which
We have come.

Into the World Beyond

The only way
To be at peace
With yourself
Is to let go
Of yourself
And let God
Take over.
We live in
A broken world,
And we ourselves
Are broken.
There is only
One place
We can turn,
Only one place
We can go.
So let us
Go there,
To the One
Who came
To us
To heal us
And redeem us
By dying for us
To express His
Love for us,
A Love
So deep that
It is presently
Unfolding
In your life and my life,
In your suffering

And my suffering,
In your death
And my death
Now and forever!
Listen to the Spirit's
Movements and promptings
In your Life!
Prepare yourself
For an adventure,
An incredible journey
Into the world beyond!

Is to Come

Night descends.
Dawn approaches.
Such is the
Movement
Of our days.
Life ends.
What are
We to make
Of what
Comes afterward?
Perhaps the pattern
Of our days
Tells us something
About the pattern
Of what
Is to come.

Life Eternal

Everything around us,
And within us,
All of Creation,
Shouts of
God's existence!
We hear this
From Creation itself,
For it resounds
Within our hearts
And reverberates
Throughout
Our entire being!
Always
And everywhere!
Yet, the sense
Of the Sacred
Has been lost
In today's world.
We embrace,
Even idolize,
Freedom,
But are enslaved
By its sacrosanct,
Unreproachable,
Autonomy.
We have
Lost ourselves
In our own
Aimless
And wandering
Self-determination.
We are

Absolutely free,
Absolutely our
Own persons!
Absolutely ourselves!
Absolutely
A people
Who can
Live life
As we please, In whatever
Which way
We choose!
But are we happy?
Are we the people
We are called to be?
Are we our deepest
And fullest selves?
Are we the persons
God envisions us
To be?
I think not.
I seriously
Think not.
Where are we
To go?
Where can
We find peace?
Where can we
Retrieve our
Lost selves
And find
Momently respite
And even
Refreshment
In a world

That has gone
Awry?
There is
Only one place,
One place
Alone, One place
That stands out!
Let us return
To that place!
Let us humbly
Place ourselves
At the feet
Of our Master,
Our Lord
Jesus Christ!
Only He
Can fill
The gaping hole
In our souls
That will
Lead us
Through
Our journey,
To True Life—
And Life Eternal!

Light My Journey

The darkness looms
And I am in need of light!
Nothing works:
No switches,
No lanterns,
No candles
No matches!
So what do I do?
I have no
Other alternative,
Than to close my eyes
And pray
In the hope
That seeing your Face
Will light my journey.

The Passing Day

Every night before I sleep
I get down on my knees
And thank God for the gift of the passing day.
I ask him to watch over me as I rest
And smile upon me as I dream.
I also ask him to accompany me
Through the night until the new day dawns,
When the rising sun will light upon the earth,
And morning beckons me from sleep,
When I will open my eyes in wonder
At the beauty of world around me
And the precious gift of another day.

My Friend

Talk to me,
If you are willing
To listen to my heart.
Walk with me,
If you are willing
To set out on an adventure.
Be with me,
If you can sit in silence
And enjoy a communion of souls.

Something New

I pour out my heart to you,
You pour out yours to me.
Our souls touch,
Our spirits intertwine—
Something new
Appears on the horizon.

So Much More

I love touching hearts
And helping them see
What was unseen
And hear what was unheard.
Words can help in doing so,
But silence and simple presence
Do so much more!

Our Evasive God

When God is present,
He is hidden.
When hidden,
Present.
We too are hidden
When present,
And present
When hidden.
And the yearning
Never ends.

The Life Beyond

There is a person,
Who is very elusive,
Yet all so very near.
Try to get to know him,
If you have not yet done so.
Please do so!
Your final happiness is at stake.
All things,
The things you cling to
Shall pass away.
This elusive person
Wishes to befriend you
And lead you into
The Life beyond.

Only You

I sense
What I
Do not see.
I wonder about
What I do not
Hear.
Only You
Can help
Me see
And hear.
Only You
Can help me
Remove
The cataracts
From my eyes
And the deep, dark wax
From my ears
That will help me
See and hear
And find my way
To You—
Only You!

Listening

We say many words,
But how many of them
Are actually heard?
Let us try
To be present
To those who speak.
Let us give them
An open ear
And a welcoming heart.
Let us be for them
As we would have liked
Them to be for us—
Listened to.
And let us remember
That, all the while,
All this great while,
Someone
Is silently,
Quietly,
And quite unobtrusively,
In the background,
Gently,
And quietly,
Listening to us.

Silence

Silence encompasses us all.
We are afraid of it
And don't wish
To confront it,
But we must.
Silence is the way
We enter
Into Eternity.
It is the way
We enter
Into ourselves
Into others,
And into God.
Without silence,
We are empty
And hollow.
Without silence
Our words
Fade away
Into insignificance.

Silence Yourself

Silence yourself.
Listen to your heart.
Breath in.
Breathe out.
Embrace the stillness.
Taste the quiet.
Feel the space around you.
Close your eyes.
Smile.
Ponder.
Imagine
Dream—
Enjoy the present moment.

Stillness

Listen to the stillness
Beneath all being.
Rest in its unassuming presence.
Hear its quiet affirmation
Of what is and is not.
Enter into its simplicity.
Utter its unuttered word.
Ponder its beauty.
Contemplate its goodness.
Embrace its wisdom—
And become its voice
In the life you live.

Solitude

To be alone
With oneself
And with God,
To reach out
To others
In one's silence,
To welcome
The silence
That we all share,
To allow the silence
To permeate oneself,
And through oneself,
To awaken the hearts
Of those you meet.

What a Gift!

I open my eyes
And am grateful
That I can see,
Breathe,
Hear,
Feel,
Touch,
Smell
And
Taste!
What a wonder
It is to be alive!
Each of us
Should be grateful
For simply
Being here,
And not there,
Or elsewhere,
Or nowhere…
What a gift!
What a glorious gift,
What a wondrous,
Glorious gift—-
To be Alive!

Reverence

Do you know
Where you
Are going?
I think I do,
But there are
So many variables
That I cannot
Be certain.
All I can say
Is that I hope
And pray
That I am
Living my life,
With God's help,
In such a way
That would give
Glory to His Name—-
And reverence
To His people.

Will You Join Me?

The tragedy of Life
Is that we fail to see
It's inner strength.
Life leads to Death.
We all know that.
But we also know
That something
Deep down
Inside of us
Yearns for something more.
That more,
That yearning,
That indescribable desire
Is what I live for!
I will never deny
Or forsake it!
It is a part
Of whom I am.
It's what makes me
The person
I have become.
It defines me!
It motivates me!
It enlivens me!
It becomes me!
There is a beyond.
I believe this
With all my
Mind, soul, heart,
And all my strength!
I am trying
To find my way there,

In my own quiet,
Haphazard way.
Will you join me?

Still We Search

Life comes
And goes.
We are born,
And we die.
We have acquaintances,
Friends and loved ones.
There are strangers
Among us as well.
We seek to give love
And receive it,
To tend it
And help it flourish,
To nourish it
And watch it grow.
Yet still we search,
Still, we want,
Still, we yearn
For someone,
To whom we
Can turn
And reveal ourselves
As we are,
Without any
Airs or pretense,
Without any masks,
Without any pretending,
Without any fear or anxiety.

Such is our search,
Our lifelong search,
Our search for acceptance,
Our search for happiness,
Our search for peace,
Our search for God.

On the Move

We are all on a journey,
Which means
We are constantly
On the move,
Always in motion.
We are nomads,
Moving from place
To place,
If not physically,
Then surely in our hearts,
And in the very
Fiber of our being.
Our hearts are restless,
For sure.
Let us listen then.
Let us listen quietly
To the promptings
Of the Spirit
Deep within our hearts,
Who touches us,
Heals us,
Speaks to us,
And points the way
For us.
Only then will
We understand
Why we are
On the move.
Only then will
We understand
That being
On the move

Is part and parcel
Of the Christian journey.

Where Are You Going?

We are all on a journey
Through this Life
And to the Life to come.
So, where are you going?
Do you think
That simply
Living Life,
However you choose,
Allows you to enter
Into Eternal Life?
If so,
I humbly ask you
To reconsider,
Because you
Are wandering
Down a path
That leads
To emptiness,
Needless suffering,
And Death.
Jesus offers
Eternal Life
To all who
Are following him.
Are you?
Are you
Really following
Him?
If not,
Then why not?
Only you
And your conscience

Knows for sure.
Repent!
Open your heart
To the Lord
And receive
His Life-Giving,
Healing Grace!
For with him
Is plentiful redemption!

Trust

I believe in Life after Death.
I believe that Jesus rose from the dead.
I believe that those who believe in Him will rise.
I believe this with all my mind
I believe this with all my heart
I believe this with all my soul.
So why am I so afraid of dying?
Why am I afraid of facing my final moment?
Why am I afraid of the unknown
Even when I believe I know what lies beyond it?
Am I afraid of what the Lord will say?
Am I afraid of the way I have lived my life?
Am I afraid of what others will say of me?
Why do I fear the unknown?
Why do I not take the Lord at His word?
"Perfect love has no fear."
"Trust me."
"Do not be afraid."
Such is Life.
Such is the human struggle.
Such is my struggle.
There are no easy answers.
I know I am lacking in love.
I know I have a long way to go.
I know I have to be forgiven.
Lord, help me to take your words to heart.
Help me to trust in your compassionate love and mercy.

The Virtues

To believe is to trust.
To hope is to yearn.
To love is to open one's heart.
When one stops opening one's heart,
Once ceases to yearn,
And ultimately one ceases to trust.

The Search

You are searching for yourself,
As I am for my own self.
There is no difference:
I am you,
And you are me.
We are all the same,
And yet so very different,
Similar,
Yet dissimilar.
Our sameness
And our differences
Distinguish us,
Yet qualify us;
Unite us,
Yet divide us;
Create discord,
Yet heal us.
Deep down within
We are all the same.
No matter what others say,
No matter what you say,
No matter what I say,
This is the Truth,
And this is my request:
That we journey together.

Our Journey

I am grateful
That we exist,
For all that
Surrounds us
I am grateful
That I exist,
Because
I am a part
Of all that is.
I am grateful
From where
I have come,
And from where
You have come.
And to where
You and I
Are going.
I am grateful
For you
Wherever
You come from.
I would like
To sit with you
Break bread
With you,
Meet with you,
And together,
Explore
Our differences,
Accept them,
Respect them,
Learn from them,

Commune with them,
As we continue
Our walk
And make our way
To our journey's
End.

Our Journey's End

There are times
When we don't
Know where
We are going,
When we
Are traveling,
But without
Direction.
Let us hope
That somehow
That direction
Will find us
And we
May be able
To continue
In search of
Our journey's
End.

To Come

The day will come
When Darkness
Will fill the Earth.
The day will come
When Hope will fall
Into the mist,
And Faith itself
Will dwindle
To a glimmer,
As will our Love
For our Lord.
The day will come
When all our hopes
Will fade
And you
Will be placed
Face-to-face
With yourself
And your Lord,
And asked
This question:
"Do you believe ?
Do you really
And truly
Believe?"
Do not take
This invitation lightly.

Your response
Will shape
The future
Of your own life
And that of
So many generations
To come.

Peace of Mind

As the sun rises
Over the horizon
And the approaching dawn,
Casts out darkness,
Announcing the beginning
Of another day,
Be resolved to face
Whatever challenges you meet
Face to face,
Eye to eye,
And toe to toe.
Only then
Will you have earned
The right,
At the coming of night,
To lay down your head
And fall asleep
With a clear conscience,
A tranquil soul,
A heartfelt prayer,
And some well-earned
Peace of mind.

Memories

Time passes slowly,
Yet Life passes by.
We have many memories,
Both good and bad,
Happy and sad.
They tell us who we are,
But do not define us.
We are more than them,
And they are less than us.
We have lived them,
And died with them.
They have shaped us,
Enlivened us,
And wounded us.
They are slices of time
We carry around with us,
Wherever we go.
They remind us
From where we came
And point to where
We are going.
Without them,
We would be lost.
With them,
We look forward
Into the future
With the hope
Of having many,
Many, many more
Such memories to come.

So Many Others

Remember from
Where you have come,
To where you are going,
And who
You are meant
To be!
Remember,
Just remember.
In time,
You will discover
What you
Are called
To be
And it,
In time,
Will manifest
Itself to you
In your life,
In your
Mind and heart,
In your own becoming,
And in the lives
Of those you touch—
And so many others,
Day in and day out.

When the Light

When the light of Life
Begins to fade,
As it already
Has for you and me,
Do not feel
Anxious,
Perplexed,
Or afraid.
The God
Who created us,
Redeemed us,
And sanctifies us,
Has already
Been through
What you are experiencing,
And more!
He has
Emptied Himself,
Given of Himself completely,
And knitted Himself
To our humanity,
And in doing so,
Welcomes us
Into His Divinity!

Yet to Come

The Time is coming
When Time,
For you and me,
Will be no more.
Let us get more
Out of the Time
That remains for us.
Let us live
In the present
As we await
The unwinding
Of our lives,
The unfolding
Of Time Itself,
And look forward
To the uncertainty
And challenges
Of what is
Yet to come.

After Easter

After the dawn of New Life,
After the celebrations
Of the Risen Life
Of Our Lord
On Easter Sunday,
After the millennia
Of practices
And Tradition,
After all
That has been said
And done,
Still,
With all
That has been
Celebrated
And yearned for,
Still,
The Lord Jesus
Confronts
Each
And every one
Of us
And asks us
To follow Him,
To love Him,
To learn from Him,
And to seek Him
In those
Around us.
He asks us
To take
Each moment

To heart,
Yes,
Moment
By moment.
There,
In the moment,
Is where
He speaks to us.
There is where
He reveals Himself.
There is where
He reveals Himself
To the deepest part
Of our souls.
So, listen,
Ask for the grace
To follow,
And never look
Back
Ask for the grace
To be
A true disciple,
Someone who
Lives in Christ
And in Christ,
Someone who
Is not afraid
To encounter
Whatever
May come.

Wherever the Spirit Leads

I have spent my life
Trying to befriend
Those around me.
I have made
Many a good friend
During this,
My earthly sojourn,
And am grateful
For each and
Every one of you,
Who has accompanied me
Along the way.
As I walk into
The twilight of my life
And face my final moments,
I hope to carry each of you
With me, in my heart,
In my mind, in my memory,
In my imagination,
In my very soul.
I am grateful for all of you
Who have journeyed with me
Throughout my life.
As I prepare for the next
Stage of my journey,
I hope to carry you with me,
Into the Beyond,
Into the Mystery
Of the Great Unknown—
Wherever the Spirit leads.

Of the Universe

There are times
when I experience
A downward pull
In Life,
One that drags
Me down
And leaves me
To wallow
In self-pity
And my own
Failures,
Sins,
And human frailties.
I find myself,
at such times,
influenced by this pull
Of becoming lesser
Rather than greater,
Of becoming
What I know
Deep down inside
What I was not
Called to be,
And what
I hoped
One day
To become.
I resist this pull
But try as I may,
I cannot overcome it.
There is only
One solution.

There is only
One answer
There is only
One Person
Who can heal me
Of my sins!
And we know
Even if unconsciously
Who that is.
There is
Little difference
Between you
And me,
Between self
And other.
Let us bow down
Before the Presence
Of the Lord,
The Creator
Of the world
And all it contains!
And open
Our hearts
To Him,
The Lord
Of the Universe!

Without Counting the Cost

We live in a world
Where there are
No holds barred!
The quest for power
Is ubiquitous!
That search
Has left us
Where we are,
Orphaned and
Derelict,
With no direction,
No path
To follow.
Listless.
Wondering what to do,
And not knowing
Where to turn!
We need to refocus,
To set our lights
On the One,
And the True,
And the Good!
We need to express
Our opinions
In the public square,
As well as in the private square!
Lord, give us the strength
To do so.

Help us to express
Our opinions
In both spheres—-
Without counting
The cost!

When You Are

When you are
In a position of authority,
Be it in a family,
Or a school,
Or a group of friends
Or a club,
Or a parish,
Or a community,
Or a school district,
Or a village,
Or a town,
Or a county,
Or a state
Or a Congressional District,
Or the Senate
Or the Supreme Court,
Or the Presidency,
Always ask yourself
How I can serve,
Rather than,
How I can promote myself.
Lead by serving others.
Lead in the Way
Of the Lord Jesus.

Your Return

We are all called to Happiness.
But what does Happiness mean?
For some, it is a transient pleasure,
For others, the possibility of greatness,
For still others, the desire for sanctity.
All these are good in themselves.
But each and every one of them
Can be the source of our own undoing,
Happiness, wholeness, holiness
Comes from our own efforts
But from God alone.
He alone can heal us.
He alone can make us whole.
He alone can make us one!
Come, Lord!
We eagerly await
Your return.

With Gratitude

It is with gratitude
That I encounter Life
And try, my best
To live it.
It is with gratitude
That I can face the day
And carry on with Life.
It is with gratitude
That I can carry on,
Day by day.
Life is difficult,
To be sure.
What will happen
Will happen,
But my soul,
My spirit,
Will carry on.
Such is the Lord's will,
And such is my will!

Mary

Mary,
Mother of Jesus,
Mother of my Lord.
You are my mother,
The mother of the Church,
And the mother of the World.
Help us!
Intercede for us!
Protect us!
Guide us!
Lead us to your Son!
Help us to follow his way,
As you did
Throughout your humble life
In Nazareth—-and beyond!